Nocturnal Animals

Primary

Save time and energy planning thematic units with this comprehensive resource. We've searched the 1990–1998 issues of **The MAILBOX®** and **Teacher's Helper®** magazines to find the best ideas for you to use when teaching a thematic unit on nocturnal animals. Included in this book are favorite units from the magazines, single ideas to extend a unit, and a variety of reproducible activities. Pick and choose from these activities to develop your own complete unit or to simply enhance your current lesson plans. You're sure to find everything you need right here in this book to unleash lots of integrated learning experiences for your students.

Editors:
Karen A. Brudnak
Kimberly Fields

Artist:
Nick Greenwood

Cover Artist:
Kimberly Richard

©2000 by THE EDUCATION CENTER, INC.
All rights reserved.
ISBN# 1-56234-345-9

Manufactured in the United States
10 9 8 7 6 5 4 3 2 1

Table Of Contents

Thematic Units

More Activities And Ideas

Reproducible Activities

Thematic Units...

from **The MAILBOX®** magazine.

The Fascinating World Of Owls

From the tops of their feathery heads to the tips of their needle-sharp talons, owls are full of fascinating surprises! Use this integrated study to investigate these remarkable raptors. There's no doubt that you and your youngsters will have a hootin' good time!

ideas contributed by Carrie Geiger, Kathleen Kopp, and Sharon Strickland

An Ancient Bird

Owls have been around for a very long time—over 50 million years! For this reason the owl is an integral part of many cultures. To some the owl is a symbol of life and good health. To others it is a symbol of bad luck, even death. Before introducing your owl study, investigate your youngsters' owl-related knowledge and beliefs. Then plan your activities so that knowledge is enhanced and beliefs are respected.

Fine-Feathered Facts

"Whooo" has the facts about owls? Your students will when you carry out this fact-sharing idea! Mount a large owl cutout in a prominent classroom location and copy the ten owl facts provided in "Have You Heard?" onto individual sentence strips. Each day post one owl fact and read it aloud. Discuss the fact as a class and, if desired, have each student copy the fact in an owl-shaped journal like the one described in "An 'Owl-some' Journal" on page 5. When all ten facts are posted, invite students to submit additional owl facts for the display. By the conclusion of your owl study, your youngsters will be all the wiser—and that's a fact!

Have You Heard?

- An owl can hear a mouse 60 feet away.
- All owl eggs are white.
- An owl has three sets of eyelids.
- Owls cannot move their eyeballs.
- An owl can turn its face upside down.
- An owl can swing its head around and look behind its back.
- Owls live on every continent except Antarctica.
- An owl can open and close its ears.
- An owl's coat is made of thousands of feathers.
- Owls use many different sounds to communicate.

Mary Lester

An "Owl-some" Journal

These student-made journals are a hoot to make and a wise place for students to record their owl-related knowledge! Give each student a white construction-paper copy of page 11. To make her journal, a student colors the owl on the page; then she carefully cuts along the dotted line that outlines the beak—stopping at the black dots. (Provide assistance with this step as needed, or you may wish to complete this step before distributing student copies.) Next the student staples a stack of 3 1/2" x 8 1/2" writing paper to the bottom of the page where indicated, folds the project forward on the thin line, and tucks the folded portion of the project under the beak flap. Lastly she adds a title and her name to the front of the project. Write on!

All About Owls By Sharon

Tip To Tip

From head to talon and wing tip to wing tip—no two kinds of owls are exactly the same! During this small-group measurement activity, students size up their arm spans and the wingspans of several owls. Post the wingspan information that is provided; then divide students into small groups. Give each group yarn, a ruler or yardstick, scissors, masking tape, and pencils.

To begin, have each student (with the help of another group member) cut a length of yarn that equals his arm span. Then have each child fold a piece of masking tape over his yarn length and label the tape with his name. Before the group members cut and label a yarn length to equal each posted wingspan, ask them to predict which wingspans will be longer or shorter than their arm spans. When the lengths are cut and labeled, have each group order its yarn lengths—wingspans and arm spans combined—from shortest to longest. Set aside time for the groups to compare their results; then, as a class, discuss the accuracy of the groups' predictions. Now that's a measurement activity that's beyond compare!

Wingspans
Barn Owl—44 inches
Great Horned Owl—60 inches
Screech Owl—22 inches
Hawk Owl—34 inches
Pygmy Owl—15 inches
Long-Eared Owl—40 inches

Night Owls

Most owls—but not all—are creatures of the night. They sleep during the day and hunt from dusk to dawn. Have students consider the advantages and disadvantages of sleeping during the day. (For a great literature connection, check your library for *The Owl And The Woodpecker* by Brian Wildsmith [Oxford University Press, 1996]. It's a delightful tale about a woodpecker and an owl who share the same forest, but not the same sleeping schedules.) Then give each child a sticky note. If a student thinks he'd rather sleep during the day, he illustrates an owl on his note. If a student likes sleeping at night, he illustrates a woodpecker or another diurnal bird. Then have each child in turn attach his illustrated note to a graph like the one shown. Summarize the graph as a class; then have students refer to the graph to answer a series of questions, like "If each night owl hoots twice when it awakes, how many hoots are heard?" and "If only seven early birds were awake when the sun rose, how many early birds overslept?"

Kind	Number										
Night Owl											
Early Bird											

Homes Around The World

Where do owls live? Just about everywhere! Owls live on every continent except Antarctica, in places like forests, deserts, fields, mountains, swamps, caves, and even cities. Their homes vary greatly, but most have one thing in common—they are not built by owls. Use the booklet project on page 12 to introduce students to six owls and their homes. To begin, give each child a white construction-paper copy of the page. Read each description aloud; then ask the students to color the habitat that is described—without coloring the owl. Next tell students that even though owls can look quite different from each other, they are usually a combination of the following colors: brown, gray, black, and white. Explain that the unique markings of each kind of owl help it blend into its natural habitat. Then challenge your students to color the owls using their newfound knowledge.

To make the booklet, each child cuts along the bold lines, pairs each scene with its matching description, and glues each pair of cutouts on a 4 1/2" x 6" rectangle of construction paper. While the glue is drying, the student folds a 6" x 9" sheet of construction paper in half to make a booklet cover. He writes "Owl Homes" and his name on the front cover; then he decorates the cover. Lastly he stacks the booklet pages, slips them inside the cover, and staples near the fold. Now that's a handy habitat reference!

Barn Owl
I might live in a barn, a cave, a tree, or an old building. I might even live in the city!

A Peek At Pellets

Scientists find looking at owl pellets a very eye-opening experience, and so will your youngsters! Remind students that owls are birds of prey, which means that they hunt and eat other animals. Also explain that owls do not have teeth, which means that they swallow their food whole or in large pieces. Because much of what an owl eats cannot be digested, several hours after eating, an owl coughs up a pellet of undigestible matter.

Tell students that scientists study pellets to learn about what owls eat; then ask your students to do the same. Give each small group of students a pellet, paper towels, plastic knives or toothpicks, and a magnifying glass. (Pellets are available from Carolina Biological Supply Company. Call 1-800-334-5551 or fax 1-800-222-7112 for ordering information.) Challenge each group to carefully pick apart its pellet to find out what kinds of items were eaten by the owl. Set aside time for each group to tell what it found, and if possible for each group to see what the other groups found in their pellets. Very interesting!

Hoot! Hoot!

Believe it or not, there are as many different owl calls as there are species of owls! This small-group activity is a fun way for youngsters to learn that owls do more than hoot! Give each small group a construction-paper strip that you have labeled with a different owl call—however, do not tell students that *all* the calls are made by owls. Allow some practice time; then have each group perform its call two or three times for the class. After each performance, tape the group's paper strip to the chalkboard and take a class vote to find out how many students believe the call is authentic (made by a real owl) or fake. Write the result of the class vote beside the paper strip. When all the calls have been made and voted on, reveal that each call is real; then, beside each call, write the name of the owl that makes it. Won't your youngsters be amazed?

Owl	Call
Screech Owl	kyew…kyew…kyew…
Pygmy Owl	whee…whee…whee…
Barn Owl	cirrrrrrrrrrr…cirrrrrrrrrrr…
Long-Eared Owl	oo-oo-oo…oo-oo-oo…
Short-Eared Owl	boo-boo-boo…boo-boo-boo…
Eagle Owl	ooo-hu…ooo-hu…ooo-hu…
Tengmalm's Owl	poo-poo-poo…poo-poo-poo…
Little Owl	hoo…hoo…hoo…hoo…hoo…

An Owlish Snack

Your owl enthusiasts are sure to enjoy making and eating these barn owl look-alikes. And it's the perfect opportunity to share a few additional facts about this unique-looking owl!

Barn Owl Look-Alikes

Ingredients:
1 slice of brown bread
1 slice of white bread
2 black olives
1 cheese triangle
peanut butter

Directions:
1. Use cookie cutters to cut a heart from the white bread and a slightly larger circle from the brown bread.
2. Use peanut butter to attach the heart shape to the center of the circle.
3. Use dabs of peanut butter to attach olive eyes and a cheese beak.

From Egg To Barn Owl

Look what just hatched—an "egg-citing" life-cycle project! Share information about the barn owl's life cycle. (In addition to the information provided, *Barn Owls* [A Carolrhoda Nature Watch Book, 1992] and See How They Grow: *Owl* [Dorling Kindersley Publishing, Inc.; 1992] are both excellent resources with outstanding photography.) Then have each student make a booklet that features a barn owl's life cycle.

To begin, a student folds a 4" x 16" strip of white construction paper in half twice; then he unfolds the paper and refolds it accordion style. Keeping the project folded, he carefully trims off each corner to create an egg-shaped booklet that resembles the white, almost-round egg of the owl. Next the student unfolds the booklet, and on the bottom half of each page describes—in sequential order—a different stage of a barn owl's life cycle. Then he illustrates each stage on the top half of its page. Lastly he refolds the booklet, writes "The Life Cycle Of The Barn Owl by [his name]" on the front cover, and draws a line to represent a crack in the egg. Students will be proud to share these adorable booklets with their families and friends!

Believe it or not, the barn owl...

- is the most common of all owls
- does not always live in a barn
- does not hoot like most owls
- often lives near humans, though humans rarely see it
- is also called the *monkey owl* because of its looks and actions
- has smaller eyes than most other owls

Life Cycle Of The Barn Owl

Stage 1: A mother owl lays one white egg every two to three days. Some barn owls lay up to 10 or 11 eggs in all.

Stage 2: After about 28 days, the eggs begin to hatch in the order they were laid. When it is first born, an owl chick has a thin coat of down and its eyes are closed. After two weeks its eyes are open and it is covered with thick, fluffy down.

Stage 3: As an owlet grows, its down is replaced by adult feathers. After about one month, an owlet becomes very active and it begins investigating outside the nest. When its wings are strong enough, it begins to practice flying. After two months the owlet can fly, but it hasn't yet developed hunting skills.

Stage 4: At 12 weeks old, a barn owl is fully feathered and able to hunt on its own.

Legendary Owls

Throughout history, people have been fascinated by owls. Many ancient legends about the owl were inspired by its unique appearance and behaviors. For example, in the legend *Why Owl Comes Out At Night* (Troll Communications L.L.C., 1996), the owl's nocturnal habits are explained. (For other books about owl legends see "Hanging Out With Owls" on page 9.) Read aloud a legend or two about the owl. Then challenge each youngster to write and illustrate a legendlike story that explains an interesting fact about the bird, like why the owl can see in the dark, why the owl can turn its head upside down, or why the owl can fly so silently. After each child has shared his work, bind the tales into a class book titled "New Legends About A Very Old Bird."

"Whooo" Cares?

Who cares about the livelihood of owls? Your students will after this important real-life lesson! Explain that at one time, farmers killed owls because some owls occasionally prey on chickens. However, farmers soon realized how important owls are in controlling rodent and insect populations. Today it is against the law to kill or capture an owl. Yet the future of many types of owls is still threatened by habitat destruction (such as the clearing of forests) and the use of insecticides.

After discussing this issue with students, inform them that there are things they can do to protect owls, such as build nest boxes for them, never use insecticides that might kill owls, and spread the word about the importance of owls. Conclude the activity by having each child decorate a construction-paper circle to create a "Give A Hoot" badge like the one shown. Then hole-punch the badges and use a safety pin to attach each child's badge to his clothing.

Give A Hoot!

insecticides that can kill owls. Cut down trees only if you have to. Spread the word that owls eat rodents. Build a nest box for an owl. Never use

All About Owls
by Carrie

Kinds Of Owls

What Owls Eat

Where Owls Live

More Facts About Owls

Step 1

Step 2

Fine-Feathered Assessment

Choose this fine-feathered (and fun!) approach to assessing your youngsters' knowledge about owls. First help each child make and label an owl-shaped flap book like the one shown (see the directions below). Then have each child write what he knows about each topic on the corresponding booklet page. "Whooooo" knew assessment could be so much fun!

Making An Owl Booklet

Step 1: Fold a 9" x 12" sheet of brown construction paper in half lengthwise and trace a template like the one shown on the folded paper. Cut on the resulting outline; then unfold the paper and set it aside.

Step 2: Stack and align the lower edges of a 9" x 12" sheet of orange paper, a 9" x 12" sheet of brown paper, and a 9" x 6" piece of yellow paper. Holding the pages vertically, slide the top sheet (yellow) upward approximately one inch and the bottom sheet (orange) downward approximately one inch. Next fold the tops of the brown and the orange sheets forward to create five graduated layers.

Step 3: Place the folded project atop the owl cutout and align the lower edges. Staple near the fold. Flip the resulting booklet over and trim the folded papers to match the shape of the cutout.

Step 4: Turn the booklet faceup. Glue beak and eye cutouts in place. Scallop the bottom of each booklet page; then label each page with a desired owl-related topic.

Hanging Out With Owls

There's no need to bundle up and head outdoors for this owling adventure! You'll find plenty of owl-related excitement between the covers of these carefully chosen books. From notable nonfiction that's packed with information to just-for-fun fiction that's simply meant to be enjoyed—we feel certain you'll have a hoot of a time!

books reviewed by Deborah Zink Roffino

Notable Nonfiction

All About Owls
Written & Illustrated by Jim Arnosky
Scholastic Inc., 1995

Jim Arnosky—wildlife enthusiast, writer of children's books, and award-winning illustrator—flawlessly fuses his talents in this beginners' guide to owls. The book's focus is on North American owls, and the information presented answers an array of questions young readers are likely to have. Arnosky even addresses owl calls and provides three commonly heard calls for practice. Detailed watercolor illustrations enhance the easy-to-understand text.

Welcome To The World Of Owls
Written by Diane Swanson
Whitecap Books, 1997

Glossy close-up photography, engaging text, and fascinating fact sidebars make this slim paperback a must for the primary classroom. Short chapters cover topics that include the habits, homes, and hoots of owls. A humorous look at the peculiarities of owls reveals that these birds are full of tricks! An elementary index for junior researchers is a great addition; however this book is most likely to be read from cover to cover!

Living Things: Owl
Written by Rebecca Stefoff
Benchmark Books, 1998

Captivating photographs lure young audiences into this intriguing investigation of owls. The primary text offers background on the physical characteristics, life cycles, and natural habitats of several owl species. In addition, six kinds of owls—including the largest and the smallest owls in the world—are spotlighted on the book's final pages.

Owls: Whoo Are They?
Written by Kila Jarvis and Denver W. Holt
Illustrated by Leslie Leroux and Courtney Couch
Mountain Press Publishing Company, 1996

Beginning with a review of the lore and superstitions surrounding owls, this appealing resource is a perfect choice for research or browsing. Colorful, authentic drawings bring clarity to the comprehensive information that is presented. An easy-to-use index and glossary enhances what is already an outstanding book for students and busy teachers.

Tiger With Wings: The Great Horned Owl
Written by Barbara Juster Esbensen
Illustrated by Mary Barrett Brown
Orchard Books, 1991

Focusing on one species, this award-winning picture book for stronger readers includes fundamental facts on the fierce great horned owl. Precise, full-color drawings invigorate the in-depth account of how this North American owl makes good use of its anatomy. The end results are a sense of wonder and deep respect for this mightiest of birds.

Birds Of The Night
Written by Jean de Sart
Illustrated by Jean-Marie Winants
Charlesbridge Publishing, Inc.; 1994

Nine owl species are examined in this unique owl resource. Each type of owl is introduced by an entertaining two-page narrative that sets the stage for an in-depth look at the remarkable raptor. Each narrative is followed by a double-page spread that features ten categories of information including location, description, size and wingspan, feathers, natural environment, and food. Elegant and detailed, the book's illustrations satisfy even the most curious of viewers.

See How They Grow: Owl
Written by Mary Ling
Photographed by Kim Taylor
Dorling Kindersley, Inc.; 1992

Chip, chip, chip! Follow the life cycle of a barn owl as it emerges from an egg, flourishes into a fluffy white owlet, and at 12 weeks old is fully feathered and almost full grown. Crystal clear, close-up photographs reveal details that will enthrall young readers. Simple, first-person text helps this heart-faced bird tell its story.

Screech Owl At Midnight Hollow

Written by C. Drew Lamm
Illustrated by Joel Snyder
Soundprints, 1996

Something mysterious is happening in a backyard at Midnight Hollow. While the setting is purely fictitious, the backyard events are packed with realism. Informative, simple sentences combine with first-class artwork to tell the story of a mother and father screech owl that are raising a nest of owlets. It's a terrific primary wildlife study that is authenticated by the Smithsonian Institution.

Whoo-oo Is It?

Written by Megan McDonald
Illustrated by S. D. Schindler
Orchard Paperbacks, 1997

Like the nocturnal world of the owl, the pages of this nighttime adventure are filled with mysterious shadows and sounds. Mother Owl recognizes, but cannot identify, the familiar soft scratching noise that she hears. Through-out the night she ponders possible sources from a raccoon climbing a tree to the flutter of a dragonfly's wings. Then, just before dawn, a tiny beak breaks the news: Mother's first owlet of the season is being born.

The Owl And The Pussycat

Written by Edward Lear
Illustrated by Jan Brett
A PaperStar Book, 1996

Brett's exquisite rendition of a Caribbean wedding between Edward Lear's prissy Pussycat and lovesick Owl is filled with intricate details and touches of humor. The colors are so daz-zling that the temperature nearly rises on the pages themselves! This fresh and gorgeous version of the beloved poem is pure paradise!

The Frightened Little Owl

Written by Mark Ezra
Illustrated by Gavin Rowe
Crocodile Books, USA; 1997

Endearing watercolor illustrations hearten this sweet tale about a young owl who is reluctant to leave the comforts of her mother's home. It is neither food nor fear that finally forces Little Owl to spread her feathery wings; it is the love she feels for her mother. And unbeknownst to Little Owl, it is her mother's love for her that prompts the high-flying events of the night.

Lazy Ozzie

Written by Michael Coleman
Illustrated by Gwyneth Williamson
Little Tiger Press, 1996

Much more clever than energetic, this laid-back owlet is determined not to fly—it just looks like too much hard work! So when Mother Owl tells her son to be on the ground by the time she returns, Lazy Ozzie tricks his barnyard pals into helping him. One fib leads to another, and soon he's outsmarted himself—but not his mother! Delightfully animated, this silly story is sure to appeal to your youngsters.

Owl Moon

Written by Jane Yolen
Illustrated by John Schoenherr
Philomel Books, 1987

The serene silence of the winter woods beckons as a fa-ther and daughter crunch over the crisp snow in search of a great horned owl. Like the young girl, readers understand that the trek is a cherished rite of passage. The dramatic mo-ment when the magnificent bird appears is keenly captured with Caldecott Medal-winning watercolor illustrations.

Hoot

Written & Illustrated by Jane Hissey
Random House, Inc.; 1997

It's the middle of the night when a menagerie of cuddly toys, led by Little Bear, investigates some unfamiliar bedroom noises. The mystery is quickly solved when a fuzzy, apron-wearing owl named Hoot swoops down for a visit. Precious, pastel illustrations and heartwarming text bring to life the re-maining events of a most memorable night.

Fold here.

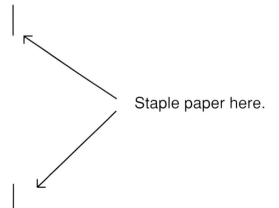

Staple paper here.

Note To Teacher: Use with "An 'Owl-some' Journal" on page 5.

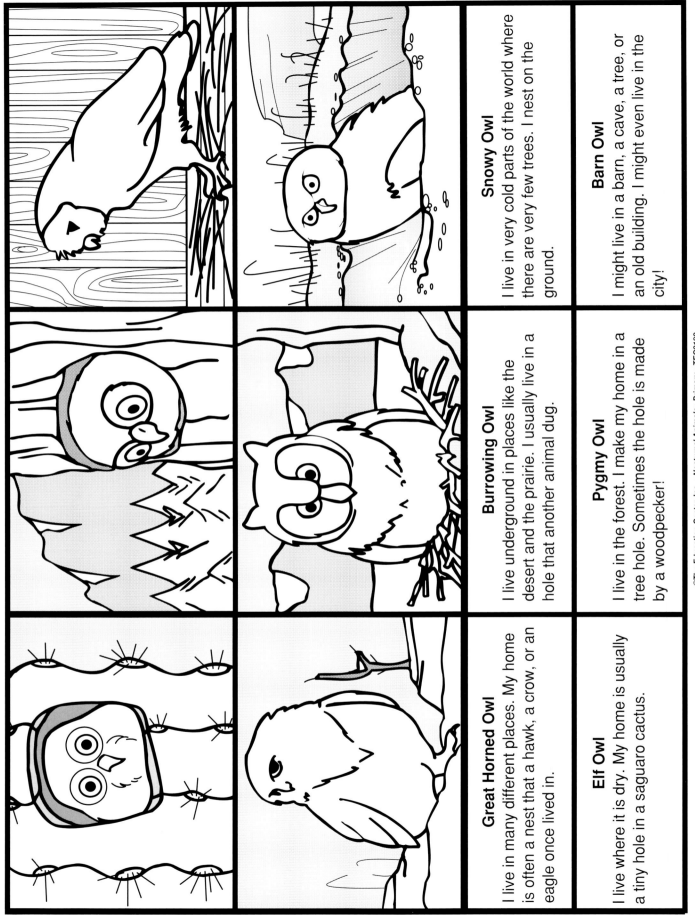

Snowy Owl
I live in very cold parts of the world where there are very few trees. I nest on the ground.

Barn Owl
I might live in a barn, a cave, a tree, or an old building. I might even live in the city!

Burrowing Owl
I live underground in places like the desert and the prairie. I usually live in a hole that another animal dug.

Pygmy Owl
I live in the forest. I make my home in a tree hole. Sometimes the hole is made by a woodpecker!

Great Horned Owl
I live in many different places. My home is often a nest that a hawk, a crow, or an eagle once lived in.

Elf Owl
I live where it is dry. My home is usually a tiny hole in a saguaro cactus.

Something To Hoot About!

Read each sentence.
If the sentence is a **fact,** color the box
   in the fact column.
If the sentence is an **opinion,** color
   the box in the opinion column.

Remember...
A **fact** can be proven.
An **opinion** is what someone thinks.

	Fact	Opinion
1. Most owls fly almost silently.	R	O
2. Owls are very strange birds.	W	L
3. Most owls hunt at night.	A	L
4. An owl has three sets of eyelids.	P	S
5. Owls are the most sneaky hunters.	A	S
6. Owls make several different sounds.	T	R
7. Owls are the wisest of all birds.	E	L
8. Owls have four toes on each foot.	O	A
9. An owl cannot turn its eyes.	R	H
10. Owls are really boring during the day.	O	C
11. Owls cannot smell.	S	O
12. Owls are more unique than all other birds.	T	F

Write the letters you did not color in order on the lines below.

— — — — —   — — — —   — —   — — — —!

Bonus Box: Read the sentence you wrote. Do you agree with this opinion? Write and explain your answer on the back of this paper.

©The Education Center, Inc. • *Nocturnal Animals* • Primary • TEC3182

Note To Teacher: Incorporate this activity into your study of owls.

13

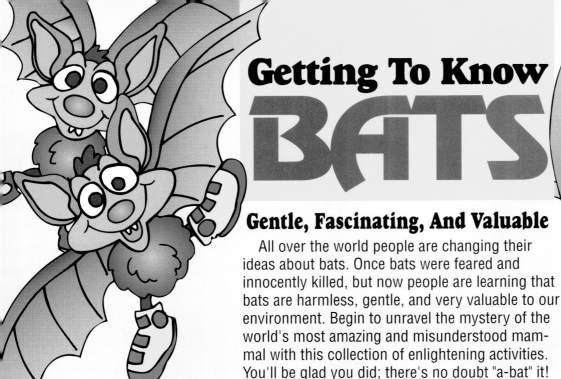

Getting To Know
BATS

Gentle, Fascinating, And Valuable

All over the world people are changing their ideas about bats. Once bats were feared and innocently killed, but now people are learning that bats are harmless, gentle, and very valuable to our environment. Begin to unravel the mystery of the world's most amazing and misunderstood mammal with this collection of enlightening activities. You'll be glad you did; there's no doubt "a-bat" it!

What's Your "Bat-itude"?

Survey your youngsters' attitudes about bats before beginning your bat study. Find out how many youngsters fear bats, have seen bats, or have heard stories about bats that they would like to share. Next have each youngster draw a picture and write a sentence that best describes his feelings about bats on a half-sheet of paper. If desired, collect and store the papers for use at the end of your bat study with "We've Flipped Over Bats!" on page 16.

Explain to students that people often confuse real bats with their make-believe counterparts. Make sure that students understand that the bats they see pictured and portrayed around Halloween are not the real thing!

Billions Of Bats

Trying to learn the names and characteristics of all the bats in the world could drive you absolutely batty! Bats make up nearly a quarter of all the mammals on earth. There are two main groups of bats and about 1,000 different species. To help young students better understand the magnitude of 1,000 different kinds of bats, challenge them as a group to collect 1,000 clean aluminum cans. Bag the cans in groups of 100; then transport them to a local recycling facility. You'll be helping the environment—something bats do every day of their lives!

Nocturnal Nametags

Youngsters are sure to go batty over these bat-shaped nametags. One can only guess what these nocturnal projects do when everyone has gone home for the day! To make a nametag, fold a 9" x 12" sheet of construction paper in half and trace the nametag pattern (page 17) onto the folded paper. Cut on the resulting outlines—not on the fold. Personalize and decorate both sides of the cutout. To complete the project, fold the tabs inward and glue one tab atop the other. When the glue is dry, adjust the folds as needed so that the resulting nametag is freestanding. Tape each student's nametag to his desk. See "The Bat 'Fact-ory' " on page 15 for a related project.

Jolene Pennington—Gr. 1–2, Hutton School, Chanute, KS

Meet The Micros

Microbats is the larger of the two bat groups. Most of the 800 bat species in this group are small, insect-eating bats that live all over the world. The eyes of microbats are small, but they can probably see as well as mice. Microbats often have large ears and unusual-looking noses that make them unattractive. However these features are an important part of the *echolocation* process which enables them to successfully prey on nocturnal flying insects.

Discuss the benefits of using bats rather than chemical insecticides to control insects. Emphasize that bats are an effective and environmentally safe means of insect control, while chemical insecticides are known to be harmful to man and the environment. For a fun cooperative group activity, have each small group create a pest control company that uses bats instead of insecticides. Have students name their companies and design logos, business cards, company trucks, employee uniforms, and advertisements for the local newspaper or radio station. Encourage each group to stress the environmental benefits that its company provides.

Meet The Megas

This smaller bat group, called *megabats* (or *flying foxes*), contains the larger bats. These large, fruit-eating bats, which resemble foxes, have large eyes and see quite well. In fact most of them do not use echolocation. These furry bats live mostly in the tropics of Asia and Africa. Unlike microbats, some megabats are active during the day.

Megabats are very important to agriculture and forestry, but their work in dispersing seeds and pollinating plants is often overlooked. Instead fruit growers complain that the bats destroy their crops. Scientists, however, have proven that these bats do not eat unripe fruit. And since most fruit growers harvest their fruit before it has ripened, it is unlikely that these bats pose a threat. More likely they are performing yet another service for the growers. By eating the ripe fruit that remains after the harvest, bats are reducing the breeding grounds and food supply of the harmful fruit fly.

To make a tasty point about the helpfulness of the fruit-eating bats, make a Fruit Bat Salad. Ask students to bring from home a variety of fruits associated with bats such as bananas, mangoes, dates, figs, avocados, and papayas. Cut up and mix the fruits together for a tasty treat. Thank you, bats!

There's No Place Like Home

Bats live in all sorts of places around the world. In fact, the only continent that bats do not inhabit is Antarctica. A bat's home or *roost* can be in a variety of places. Some bats live in caves, some live in treetops, and others live deep in hollow logs. In India there are even bats that live underground with porcupines! Many other bat roosts are in the nooks and crannies of castles, churches, and homes. Amazingly enough, one bat may have a dozen or more roosts.

Ask youngsters how they might feel if bats moved into their homes. Explain that once people in Europe thought that it was unlucky for bats to enter their homes, while people in China welcomed the visitors because they supposedly brought good luck. For a fun creative-writing project, have students write and illustrate stories about bats that move into their homes. Encourage students to write about where the bats made their roosts, how their families liked the batty visitors, and what kinds of luck (if any) the bats brought with them. Be sure to provide time for students to share their creative tales.

The Bat "Fact-ory"

To entice further interest in bats, display this sampling of amazing bat facts. After reading and discussing each one, have students copy the facts onto individual 1 1/2" x 9" construction-paper slips. For nifty storage, have students slip the fact strips inside their bat-shaped nametags. (See "Nocturnal Nametags" on page 14.) Keep a supply of colorful construction-paper strips and a variety of bat-related resources on hand so that students can add to their bat fact collections. Each day invite students to share any new bat facts they have discovered. At the end of the project, help each youngster bind his fact strips together using a brad of the appropriate size. Now that's a handy reference of batty facts!

Amazing But True
- One type of bat scoops fish out of water.
- Fruit-eating bats help spread tree seeds in rain forests.
- Bat waste is called *guano* and is a valuable fertilizer.
- Bats are a tourist attraction in Austin, Texas.
- The smallest mammal on earth is the bumblebee bat of Thailand. It weighs less than one penny.

Brushing Up On Bats

Is that a fact? Give youngsters an opportunity to showcase their fact and opinion skills with this ready-to-use activity. Copy pages 18 and 19. Glue page 19 onto the front of a 9" x 12" string-tie envelope. Laminate page 18; then cut out the cards and answer key. Store the cards and answer key inside the envelope. A student removes the contents of the envelope and sets the answer key aside (facedown) before he reads and sorts the cards on top of the gameboard. Then he uses the answer key to check his work.

If desired, enlist your youngsters' help in reprogramming the center. Duplicate a supply of the open game cards on page 20. Divide students into small groups, and instruct each group to program additional fact and opinion cards and a corresponding answer key. Prepare the cards and answer key as described above and place them in the empty envelope.

adapted from an idea by Kathleen Knoblock, Torrance, CA

Bat Conservation International

For bats, conservation cannot begin without education, which is a major focus of Bat Conservation International. For information about bat-related teaching materials, call 1-800-538-BATS, check out www.batcon.org, or write to:

Bat Conservation International
P.O. Box 162603
Austin, TX 78716

We've Flipped Over Bats!

For an eye-opening culminating activity, have students repeat the activity described in "What's Your 'Bat-itude'?" on page 14. This time, instead of collecting the papers, redistribute the youngsters' work from the first activity. Invite students to share how their feelings about bats have changed (if appropriate).

For added fun, have each student prepare his project for display at a bulletin board entitled "We've Flipped Over Bats!" To prepare a project, fold in half a colorful sheet of 9" x 12" construction paper and mount one paper to each side of the folded paper. (The lower edge of each paper should be positioned near the fold.) Using a tagboard tracer of the pattern on page 17, trace and cut out a bat shape from a 6" x 9" sheet of construction paper. Decorate both sides of the cutout; then position and glue or staple the tab between the open ends of the folded project. Use lengths of yarn to suspend the projects from pushpins inserted into the bulletin board. "Battacular"!

A Real Batman

Merlin D. Tuttle has rightly earned the title of "batman." Founder of Bat Conservation International, Dr. Tuttle has led the drive to reeducate people with the truth about bats. Tuttle's fascination with bats began almost by accident. Although he was interested in nature at an early age, it was not until he was in high school that bats piqued his curiosity. In fact if his family had not moved to Knoxville, Tennessee, about two miles from a bat cave, Tuttle may not have been so intrigued by these strange creatures. *Batman: Exploring The World Of Bats* (Charles Scribner's Sons Books For Young Readers) gives a captivating account of Tuttle's life and accomplishments, as well as a wealth of amazing bat information. This book is out of print, so check your library for a copy

Have youngsters support Tuttle's efforts and spread the real facts about bats. Duplicate student copies of the badge pattern on page 17. To make the badges, have students color and cut out the badge patterns, then glue them atop slightly larger construction-paper circles. To wear the badges, have each student use a hole punch to punch a hole near the top of his badge, then thread a length of yarn through the hole and tie the yarn ends. Or use a safety pin to attach the badge to each youngster's clothing.

I learned that bats are gentle and good for the environment.
Katie

Use with "A Real Batman" on page 16.

I'm
BATTY
about bats!

Please ask me
about them!

Place on fold.

Place on fold.

tab

Use with "Nocturnal Nametags" on page 14.

Also use with "We've Flipped Over Bats!" on page 16. (For this project, disregard the programming on the pattern.)

1. Seeing a bat is a lucky sign.

2. All bats are mammals.

3. Flying foxes are the largest bats.

4. Some bats eat fruit.

5. Bats are more interesting than spiders.

6. Bats are active at night.

7. A bat would make a fun pet.

8. Bats are ugly.

9. Bats are the most useful to farmers.

10. Bats are the only mammals that fly.

11. Some bats hibernate.

12. Bats fly very fast.

13. Bats look funny hanging upside down.

14. Bats are important to our environment.

15. Good hearing is more important than good sight.

16. Bats should live far away from people.

17. Bat caves are spooky.

18. All bats do not look alike.

Answer Key

Fact Cards
2, 3, 4, 6, 10, 11, 12 14, 18

Opinion Cards
1, 5, 7, 8, 9, 13, 15, 16, 17

Brushing Up On BATS

Sort the cards.
Use the answer key to check your work.

Facts About Bats

Opinions About Bats

Note To Teacher: Use with "Brushing Up On Bats" on page 16.

Open Game Cards

Use with "Brushing Up On Bats" on page 16.

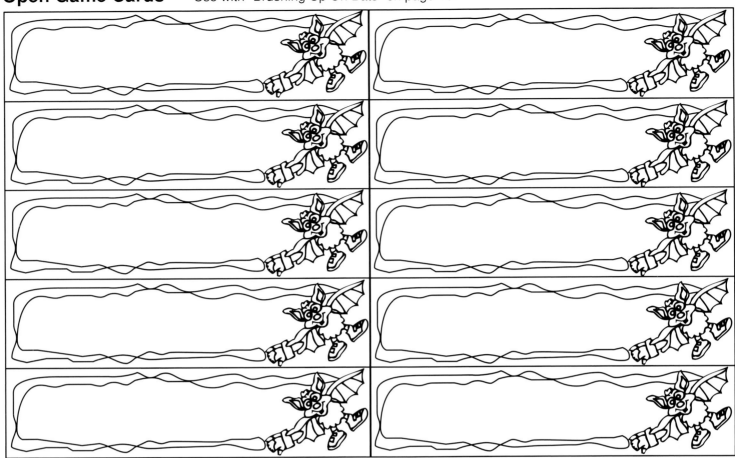

Awards

Duplicate and present the awards to students as desired.

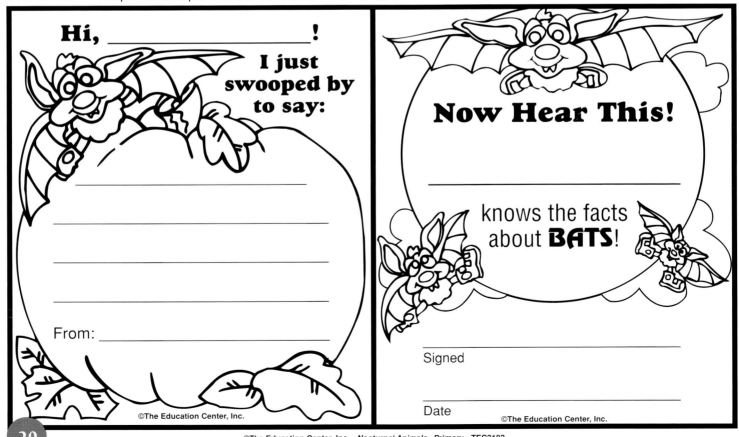

Hi, _____!

I just swooped by to say:

_____
_____
_____
_____

From: _____

©The Education Center, Inc.

Now Hear This!

_____

knows the facts about **BATS**!

_____
Signed

_____
Date

©The Education Center, Inc.

A Pocketful Of Science

Bats And Sound

Bats are equipped in remarkable ways to hunt at night. They use sound waves and a technique called *echolocation.* Using these activities, you can further explore the uniqueness of these nocturnal creatures and introduce the basic principles of sound.   *ideas by Ann Flagg*

Activity 1: Vibrations

You will need:
one large rubber band per student

What to do:
Have youngsters firmly grasp one end of their rubber bands in each hand, then release their index fingers and thumbs. Then, using their thumbs and index fingers, have students pluck and strum their rubber bands to make a variety of sounds. Instruct students to carefully watch their rubber bands as they listen to the sounds being made.

Questions to ask:
1. Were all of the sounds you made alike?
2. What was the rubber band doing when you heard a sound?

Next:
Have each child place his fingers on the bony part of his throat; then lead students in a chorus of sounds. For example say, "Ahhhhhh," "Eeeeeee," and "Mmmmmmm." Have each student describe to a classmate what he felt with his fingers. Then have each child invent a sound of his own and describe what he felt.

Questions to ask:
1. What did you feel when you said, "Ahhhhhh," and touched your throat?
2. Did all of the sounds you made feel the same to your fingers?
3. Think about the rubber band. What do you think might be happening inside your throat when you talk, sing, or make other sounds?

This is why:

Sound is given off when something vibrates. A person's vocal cords vibrate like rubber bands across a voice box. When you touch the bony part of your throat (the Adam's apple) and make a sound, you can feel the vibrations of the vocal cords.

Activity 2: Sound Waves

You will need:
glass pan or clear plastic container filled with one inch of water
food coloring (optional)
eyedropper full of water
overhead projector

What to do:
If desired, use the food coloring to tint the water. Place the pan of water on the overhead projector and project the watery image. When the water becomes calm, use the eyedropper to drop a droplet of water into the pan. Repeat this procedure.

Questions to ask:
1. What did you see when each water droplet fell into the pan of water?
2. What happened when the water waves reached the sides of the pan?

This is why:

Although we cannot see sound waves, the circular waves that were seen in the water are similar to how sound waves travel through the air. When the water waves bounced off the sides of the pan and moved back towards the middle, you saw how an echo is formed. (When you hear an echo, your sound waves have hit and bounced off a very hard surface, and then traveled back to you!)

Pam Crane

Activity 3: Extraordinary Hearing

You will need:
a selection of music and a method of playing it
student copies of page 23

What to do:
Distribute the student activity pages and ask youngsters to study the bats pictured. Explain that bats are amazing nighttime hunters; then ask students to brainstorm reasons why this might be so. Next play the music and ask students to listen carefully. Keep the music volume low. After several seconds, turn the music off. Have youngsters cup their hands and place one cupped hand behind each of their ears. Keeping their hands cupped, have students gently extend each ear, bringing their outer ears forward. In this position, have students listen to the same selection of music again.

Questions to ask:
1. Did you notice a difference in the music when you listened to it the second time? If so, what was the difference?
2. Why do you think the music sounded louder?
3. How might a bat's large ears help make it a better hunter?

This is why:

Sound travels through the air in waves, which spread out in all directions (see Activity 2). When students listened to the music the first time, a few sound waves reached their ears, but most of the waves bypassed their ears and traveled across the room. When the students' ears were cupped, more sound waves were captured and channeled to their ears. This made the music sound louder. Bats' ears are large and cupped, therefore much more efficient than human ears. Bats can hear and capture a tiny mosquito in complete darkness! In fact, using echolocation (see Activity 4), a bat can catch as many as 600 mosquitoes in one hour!

Next:
Have each student complete his activity sheet by drawing and illustrating a bat as described.

Activity 4: Echolocation

You will need:
a blindfold

What to do:
Use this large-group game to simulate echolocation. To introduce the game, explain that bats use sound waves, echoes, and their amazing ears to catch tiny insects and moths at night. Then have students form a large circle in an open area. Blindfold one child (the bat) and lead her to the center of the circle. Appoint several other youngsters to be moths and ask them to step inside the circle. Have the remaining students evenly space themselves around the circle and act as trees. To play, the bat and the moths carefully move around inside the circle. The bat repeatedly calls out in a high squeaky voice, "Moth?" and the moths, using loud voices, repeatedly answer, "Moth!" The object of the game is for the bat to listen carefully and tag as many moths as possible within an allotted amount of time. When a moth is tagged, she becomes a tree. If the bat wanders too close to the edge of the circle, the trees nearby whisper, "Tree! Tree!" and carefully help steer the bat back on course. (Whispering keeps the trees from overpowering the moths.) Play as many rounds of the game as desired.

Questions to ask:
1. Why must the bat call out?
2. Why must the moths respond each time the bat calls out?

This is why:

Bats make rapid squeaking sounds that are usually too high-pitched for human ears to hear. If an insect is flying near a bat, these sounds bounce off the insect and echoes are heard by the bat. (In the game the moths' responses simulated these echoes.) The resulting echoes inform the bat how far away the insect is, as well as the shape and size of the insect. This is called echolocation. Bats avoid trees and other obstacles in the same manner. Because echolocation is so important to bats, they are constantly flying around with their mouths open making squeaking noises. Since people cannot hear the sounds, they often mistake a bat's open mouth as a sign of aggression, when in fact it is only navigating.

The Incredible Bat

Bats are excellent nighttime hunters.
Look at each bat face below.

1.
Caribbean White Bat

2.
Spear-Nosed Bat

3.
Slit-Faced Bat

Remember how a bat hunts.
Draw and color a new kind of bat that will be a great hunter.
Write its name on the line.

_____

Note To Teacher: Use this activity with "Activity 3: Extraordinary Hearing" on page 22.

Bright Ideas About

Hoot Owls

Here's an art project that won't ruffle any feathers! To make an owl, fold and glue three corners of a 9" brown paper square so that they touch in the center of the paper. For tail feathers, use scissors to fringe the unfolded corner. Gently pull some of the fringes forward and some backward for dimension. For the owl's beak, fold a 1 1/2" orange paper square in half diagonally and glue it on. For eyes, cut two 2 1/2" yellow paper circles and two 2 3/4" black paper circles. Glue each yellow circle atop a black one. Use a black marker to make a pea-size dot in the center of each yellow circle before gluing each eye in place. Create a spooky spectacle by displaying your youngsters' owls perched on a bare tree cutout.

Bat Mobiles

Your classroom will have more bats than a belfry when these mobiles are flitting to and fro in schoolroom breezes. Without changing the shape of the hook or the bottom part, gently bend both sides of a coat hanger downward. Place the hanger near the upper edge of a half-sheet of black tissue paper. Squeeze a thin trail of glue around the hanger; then fold up the lower half of the paper all the way around the hanger. The following day, trim the excess paper from the hanger. For wings, glue a few tissue paper strips on each side of the hanger. Complete the mobile by gluing on additional paper features.

To vary this idea, bend a coat hanger into a ghostlike shape. Using a whole sheet of white tissue paper, complete the ghost similarly to the bat.

Cecile Shetler—Gr. 3
Louisiana State University Laboratory School
Baton Rouge, LA

Night Creatures • • • • •

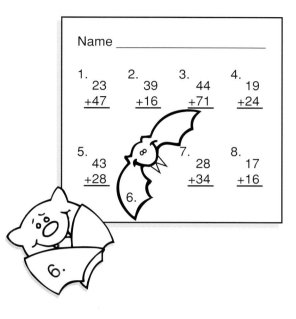

Name _____

1.
23
+47

2.
39
+16

3.
44
+71

4.
19
+24

5.
43
+28

6.

7.
28
+34

8.
17
+16

Bat Math!

Students will go batty over this math activity! Write an assortment of numbered math problems on a student reproducible. Draw bat shapes intermittently between the problems. Label each bat shape with a number. Photocopy a sheet for each child. Around the room, display a matching number of bat cutouts. Label the center of each cutout with a number and a direction to follow, such as: tell one fact about bats to a friend, flap your wings and fly like a bat back to your desk, or see your teacher for a batty treat. Fold the wings of each cutout over its programming. Have students complete the math problems in order. When a student comes to a bat outline, he must locate its corresponding cutout in the room. He then follows the directions on the cutout before returning to his desk to continue working on his remaining math problems. This idea can easily be adapted to other animal studies.

Janine Sutko—Gr. 2, Rockwell Elementary, Omaha, NE

Batty Bookmarks

These projects are no fly-by-night whimsies. They're bookmarks to mark the pages of the books that your youngsters are batty about! To make a bookmark, begin by cutting one 2" x 9" strip of paper. From a contrasting color of paper, cut another strip measuring 1 1/2" x 8". Glue the smaller strip to the larger strip so that the top margin is slightly larger than the bottom and side margins. Cut two 2-inch circles from black paper. Use a hole puncher to punch three holes in one of the circles for the eyes and mouth of a bat. (Punch the eyeholes near the circle's edge.) Glue this circle to the top of the bookmark. Position the circle so that one color shows through the eye holes and another through the mouth hole. (Trim off the portion of the bookmark that extends above the circle.) Using a zigzag cut, cut along the diameter of the remaining circle. Accordion-fold each resulting shape, and glue it to the bat body for a wing. Complete the bat bookmark by adding pupils and tiny fangs with a fine-tip marker.

For a more intricate bookmark, first fold the smaller strip in half lengthwise. Then, cutting from the folded edge, cut a few shapes from the strip. (Leave approximately 1/2 inch at the top end of the strip uncut.) Unfold the paper and glue it to the larger strip as described above; then finish the project as before.

Give A Hoot!

Attract parents to Open House festivities or parent conferences with these adorable, student-made owl magnets. Flatten a small portion of baking dough (see recipe below) to approximately 1/2-inch thickness. Cut a circle 2 inches in diameter from the dough for the owl face. (Use the pattern below or press an inverted plastic glass of a similar size into the dough.) Pull away the excess dough; then use your thumb and index finger to pinch two eye sockets into the center of the circle. Brush lightly with egg (to achieve a golden color while baking) and bake in a 300° oven until hardened (approximately one hour). When cool, use tempera paint to create an orange triangular beak and white eye sockets. When dry, securely fasten a wiggle eye in each socket.

Duplicate the remaining owl patterns onto tagboard, cut out, and use as tracers to transfer each pattern onto appropriate colors of tagboard. Assemble the owl body as shown. Use a hot glue gun to affix the face and a magnetic strip to the owl body. Personalize the owl as desired. Display the owl magnets during Open House or parent conferences along with a note to each parent from his child. Have parents place the magnets on their home refrigerators to display their children's work.

Kenneth T. Helms—Gr. 3
Irving Park School
Greensboro, NC

Baking Dough Recipe
2 cups flour   water
1 cup salt
Mix enough water with the dry ingredients to make a dough.

Look what Valerie did!

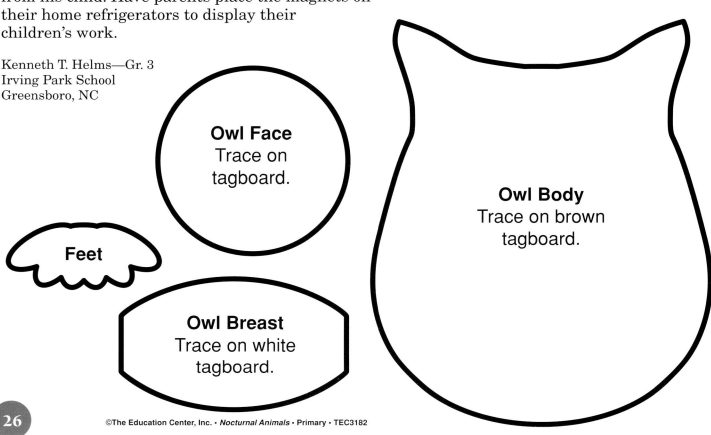

Owl Face
Trace on tagboard.

Feet

Owl Breast
Trace on white tagboard.

Owl Body
Trace on brown tagboard.

Reproducible Activities...

from **Teacher's Helper**® magazine.

Materials Needed For
Each Student:
— 1 construction-paper copy of each of these pages: 29,
   31, 32, and 33, prepared as directed
— 1 copy of the booklet patterns on page 30
— one 8" x 12" piece of black construction paper
— 1 pencil
— crayons
— scissors
— glue
— tape
— 4–6 gummed foil stars
— 2 wiggle eyes (1 cm diameter)
— 1 photocopy of a school photo or some other picture

You Will Need:
— X-acto® knife
— paper cutter

How To Use Pages 29–33 To Make
A Night Creatures Booklet

1. To prepare the copies of page 29 for student use,
   use an X-acto® knife to cut along the dotted circles
   where the child's face is on the booklet covers. Use
   a paper cutter to cut pages 29, 30, 31, and 32
   along the broken lines.

2. To begin the **booklet backing**, instruct each child
   to color the moon yellow and cut along the heavy
   solid outline. Have him glue the backing to the black
   construction paper, leaving a 1 3/4" black margin at
   the top. Have each child stick his gummed foil stars
   to the black paper above the moon.

3. To complete the **booklet cover**, have each child
   write his name where indicated and color as desired. Help each child tape his photo behind the
   circular cutout so that his photo can be seen when
   looking at the booklet cover. Have each child cut
   out the cover along the heavy solid outline and set
   it aside for later assembly. Begin discussing traits
   of nocturnal animals using the "Background For
   The Teacher: Nocturnal Animals" on page 30.

4. To complete **booklet page 1**, read the text aloud
   and discuss the characteristics of bats. Then have
   each child write the word *insects* to complete the
   sentence. Instruct each child to color the bat and
   the bat wings (see the booklet patterns). Have him
   cut out the bat wings and glue them where indicated. Ask each child to draw three bugs near the
   bat. Have him cut out the page along the heavy
   solid outline and set it aside for later assembly.

5. To complete **booklet page 2**, read the text aloud
   and discuss the characteristics of raccoons. Then
   have each child write the word *people* to complete

the sentence. Instruct each child to color the
raccoon and the raccoon tail (see the booklet
patterns). Have him cut out the tail and glue it where
indicated. Ask each child to draw yellow stars in the
sky. Have him cut out the page along the heavy solid
outline and set it aside for later assembly.

6. To complete **booklet page 3**, read the text aloud and
   discuss the characteristics of moths. Then have each
   child write the word *flowers* to complete the sentence.
   Instruct each child to color the moth and the moth
   wings (see the booklet patterns). Have him cut out the
   wings, place a dot of glue on the X, and then attach the
   wings. Have each child cut out the page along the
   heavy solid outline and set it aside for later assembly.

7. To complete **booklet page 4**, read the text aloud and
   discuss the characteristics of toads. Then have each
   child write the word *sticky* to complete the sentence.
   Instruct each child to draw the frog's tongue catching
   the fly. Have each child cut out the page along the
   heavy solid outline and set it aside for later assembly.

8. To complete **booklet page 5**, read the text aloud and
   discuss the characteristics of owls. Then have each
   child write the word *heads* to complete the sentence.
   Instruct him to color the owl and glue the wiggle eyes
   on the owl's face. Ask each child to draw yellow stars
   in the sky. Have each child cut out the page along the
   heavy solid outline.

9. To complete the booklet, have each child draw and
   color his favorite night creature on the booklet backing. Then have him sequence the booklet cover and
   pages atop the booklet backing where indicated.
   Staple along the left-hand margin.

My Book About
Night Creatures

by _____

1

Bats fly at night.

They can't see well in the dark.

They use their voices and ears to find their way.

_____

_____

Bats eat many _____.

Background For The Teacher
Nocturnal Animals

As we settle down to sleep each night, a whole world of animals is just waking up. Nocturnal animals are active during the nighttime hours—looking for food, communicating with one another, and caring for their young. The dark of night provides these animals with safety from predators; hot, dry conditions; and other animals competing for food. Many nocturnal animals have developed keen senses to help them function in their dark environments.

Bats are the only mammals with wings. They find their way in the dark using a system called *echolocation*—listening for sound waves from their voices that bounce off objects in their path. Bats are important in keeping the insect population down. One bat can eat as many as 600 mosquitoes an hour!

Raccoons flourish because they will eat almost anything. From insects and frogs to kitchen scraps, these scavengers aren't likely to go hungry. Raccoons' diets often reflect the seasons. Spring brings fresh eggs from nests while fall offers nuts, berries, and insects.

Moths use the moon to navigate. A lightbulb can be mistaken for the moon, causing moths to fly right into it. Moths are insects—relatives of butterflies—that feed on nectar from flowers. A moth's antennae are used like a nose and fingers; they are used to sense food or a mate.

Toads spend most of the year on land. They return to the ponds only to mate and lay eggs. Because their skin must remain damp, they avoid the hot, dry conditions of daytime. Toads wait for food to come near them; then they quickly catch it with their long, sticky tongues.

Owls, unlike most birds, have excellent night vision. In fact their eyes are so large that there's no room for muscles to move them. Instead owls are able to rotate their heads to provide complete sight. Owls also have keen hearing that allows them to hunt in almost complete darkness.

Related Literature
Nocturnal Animals

Beautiful Bats
Written by Linda Glaser
Illustrated by Sharon Lane Holm
Published by The Millbrook Press, Inc.; 1997

Night Creatures
Written by Susanne Santoro Whayne
Illustrated by Steven Schindler
Published by Simon & Schuster Books For Young Readers, 1993

Booklet Patterns

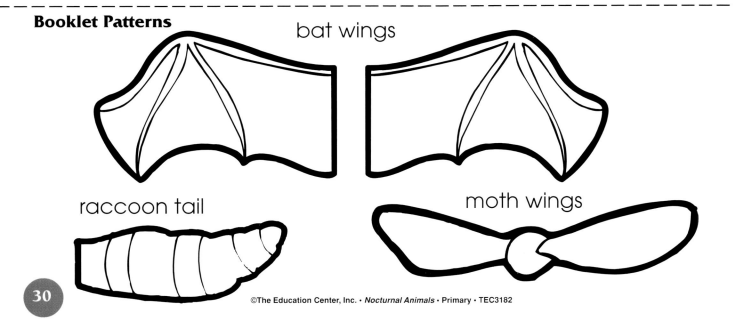

bat wings

raccoon tail

moth wings

2

Glue.

Raccoons sleep during the day.
They look for food at night.
They eat many different foods.

_____

_ _ _ _ _ _ _ _ _ _ _ _ _ _ _ _ _

Some raccoons live near _____.

3

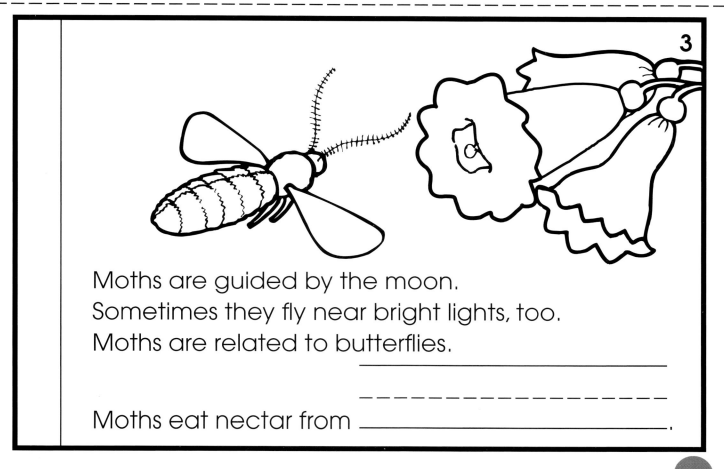

Moths are guided by the moon.
Sometimes they fly near bright lights, too.
Moths are related to butterflies.

_____

_ _ _ _ _ _ _ _ _ _ _ _ _ _ _ _ _

Moths eat nectar from _____.

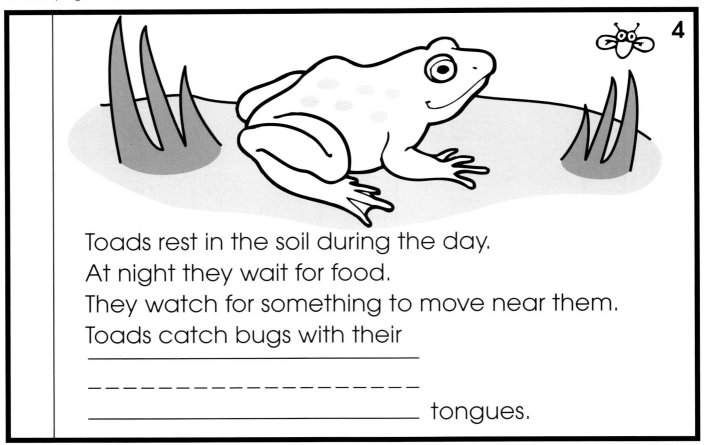

4

Toads rest in the soil during the day.
At night they wait for food.
They watch for something to move near them.
Toads catch bugs with their

_____

_ _ _ _ _ _ _ _ _ _ _ _ _ _ _ _ _ _ _

_____ tongues.

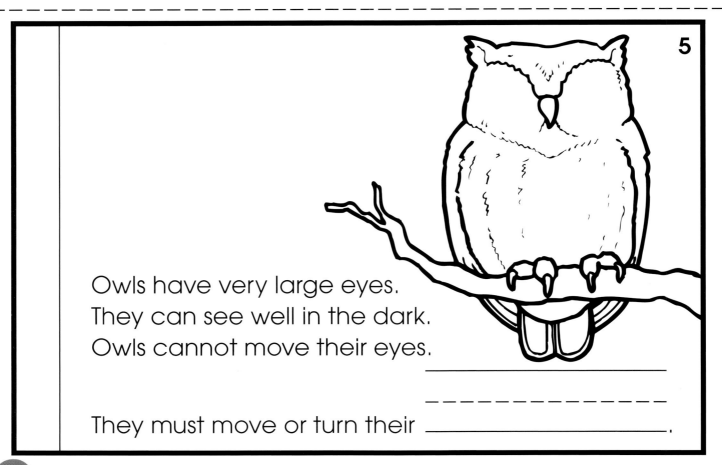

5

Owls have very large eyes.
They can see well in the dark.
Owls cannot move their eyes.

_____

_ _ _ _ _ _ _ _ _ _ _ _ _ _ _ _ _

They must move or turn their _____.

Staple pages here.

This is my favorite night creature.

Background For The Teacher
Owls

Owls are powerful birds of prey that exist by eating other animals. Hooked beaks, strong claws, and superkeen senses make owls skillful hunters. They live on every continent except Antarctica and occupy a wide variety of habitats that include forests, deserts, prairies, and even the Arctic tundra. Owl homes vary as well. Some owls live in trees, while others live on or under the ground. Owls seldom build their own nests, but once an owl finds a nest to occupy, it fiercely defends it.

Scientists have identified about 145 different owl species. The smallest owl species, the *elf owl,* measures about six inches long. The largest species, the *great gray owl,* measures about 30 inches long and has a wingspan of almost twice its length. Most owls are nocturnal, meaning that they hunt at night. One exception is the elf owl, which hunts during the day.

Hooting is the sound most often associated with owls, but these skillful hunters use many different sounds to communicate. Whistles, screams, shrieks, trills, barks, and squeals are just some of the sounds made by owls!

How To Use Pages 34–41

Give your youngsters something to hoot about with this thematic collection of owl-related reproducibles. "Whooooo'd" know that owls could make comparing numbers, making compound words, forming plurals, using homonyms, and creating glyphs so much fun! To learn more about these wondrous creatures of the night, refer to "Background For The Teacher: Owls" on this page.

Answer Key For Page 35

1. 95
2. 17
3. 59
4. 83, 71
5. <u>26</u> < 32
   <u>62</u> > 45
6. 40 > 34
7. Answers will vary.
8. <u>[Answer to #7]</u> < 78

Bonus Box Answers:
95, 83, 71, 62, 59, 40, 34, 26, 17,
[Answer to #7]

Answer Key For Page 41

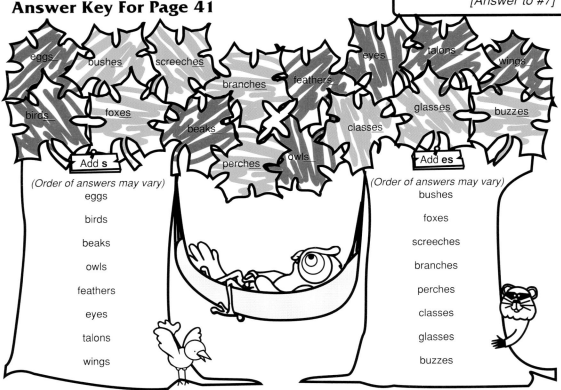

Add s
(Order of answers may vary)
eggs
birds
beaks
owls
feathers
eyes
talons
wings

Add es
(Order of answers may vary)
bushes
foxes
screeches
branches
perches
classes
glasses
buzzes

Name_____

"Whoooooo's" Stargazing?

Answer the problems in order.
Write your answers on the lines.
Use each number only one time.
When you use a number,
color its star yellow.

26 34 40
71
59   17
95   83 62

Hooty's Home

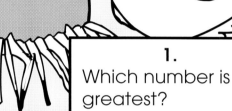

1. Which number is greatest? _____	2. Which number is least? _____	3. Which number is greater than 48 and less than 61? _____
4. Which two numbers are less than 90 and greater than 62? _____ _____	5. Complete each number sentence. _____ < 32 _____ > 45	6. Two numbers remain. Use them to complete this sentence. _____ > _____
7. Write a number in the blank star that is less than the other numbers.	8. Use the remaining number to complete this math sentence. Draw a symbol in the circle. _____ ◯ 78	**Bonus Box:** Use the ten numbers on the stars. Write them from greatest to least on the tree trunk.

Materials Needed For Each Student:

— white construction-paper copy of page 37
— white construction-paper copy of the eye patterns below
— crayons or markers
— scissors
— two brad fasteners
— pencil

Directions For Each Student To Make An-Eye-To-Eye Owl

1. Color the owl pattern, leaving the owl's tummy white.
2. Cut out the pattern; then carefully cut on the dotted lines to create a window between the owl's eyes. *(Provide assistance as needed.)*
3. Cut out the left and the right eye patterns.
4. To attach the left eye pattern, poke a brad through the center dot of the owl's left eye; then poke the brad through the center dot of the eye pattern labeled "L."
5. To attach the right eye pattern, poke a brad through the center dot of the owl's right eye; then poke the brad through the center dot of the eye pattern labeled "R."
6. Complete the activity by following the provided directions.

Completed Project

Turn the wheel behind each eye to make compound words.

Write the compound words you make on the lines.

Name _Cassidy_

1. sunshine
2. cowboy
3. eyelash
4. butterfly
5. cupcake
6. snowflake
7. fingernail
8. classmate
9. sidewalk
10. mailbox

Hint: When a compound word appears in the window, the symbols match.

Eye Patterns

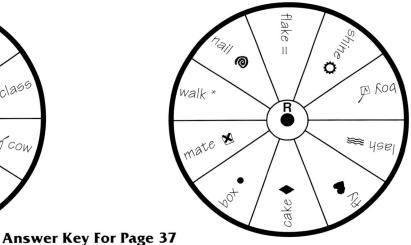

Left Eye

Right Eye

Answer Key For Page 37

(Order of answers will vary.)

1. classmate
2. fingernail
3. cowboy
4. butterfly
5. sunshine

6. snowflake
7. cupcake
8. mailbox
9. eyelash
10. sidewalk

Eye To Eye

Cut out.

Turn the
wheel behind
each eye
to make
compound
words.

Write the
compound
words you
make on
the lines.

Name _____

1. _____

2. _____

3. _____

4. _____

5. _____

6. _____

7. _____

8. _____

9. _____

10. _____

Hint: When a compound word appears in
the window, the symbols match.

37

Owls Across The Curriculum

Assembled Project

Materials Needed For Each Student:
— light tan or cream construction-paper copy of page 39
— crayons
— scissors
— glue

How To Use Page 39
Explain to students that a *glyph* is a picture or a symbol that conveys information. Tell students that they are going to make owl glyphs that will reveal information about themselves. Then distribute the materials listed above. Give the following directions.

Directions For Each Student To Make A One-Of-A-Kind Owl

1. Color each pattern on page 39 by listening carefully to the following directions:

   Body: Color brown if you prefer warm weather.
   Color white if you prefer cool weather.

   Wings: Color brown and white if you prefer reading over math.
   Color brown and black if you prefer math over reading.

   Facial Discs: Color black if you do not like cartoons.
   Color white if you like cartoons.

   Eyes: Color yellow if you have a sister.
   Color blue if you have a brother.
   Color green if you have a brother and a sister.

   Beak: Color red if you like to sing.
   Color yellow if you like to draw.
   Color orange if you like to sing and draw.

   Ear Tufts: Color white if you do not have a pet.
   Color black if you have a pet.

   Feet: Color orange if you prefer pizza over tacos.
   Color red if you prefer tacos over pizza.

2. Cut out the patterns.
3. Glue each eye cutout to a facial disc.
4. Glue the ear tufts, the facial discs, and the beak, to the body.
5. Glue the feet to the body. Leave space between the feet if you like to skate.
6. Glue the wings to the body. If you like ice cream, show the wings extended as if the owl is flying.

Follow-Up Activities
— Pair students and have each student use his owl glyph to tell his partner about himself. Then ask each child to find a different partner and repeat the activity.

— Have each child write his name near the bottom or on the back of his project. Then collect and display the students' work on a bulletin board titled " 'Whoooo' Can Tell?" Each day post a different question of the day that can be answered by studying the owl glyphs. Questions might include "How many students prefer reading over math?" and "How many students own pets?" To increase the difficulty level, post two-step questions, such as "How many of the students who like to skate also prefer pizza over tacos?" and "How many students who have both a brother and a sister like to sing and draw?"

Answer Key For Page 40

1. Dear	9. some
2. new	10. eight
3. sees	11. for
4. hole	12. creek
5. know	13. week
6. would	14. fir
7. sun	15. red
8. so	16. berry

Name_____

A One-Of-A-Kind Owl

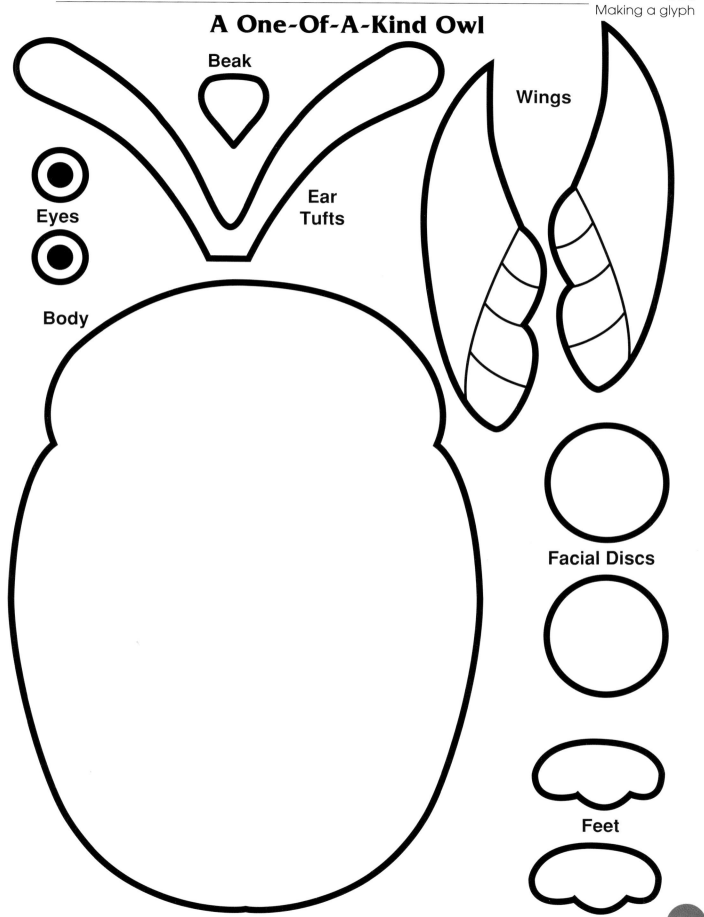

Beak

Wings

Eyes

Ear
Tufts

Body

Facial Discs

Feet

Name_____

New Home Needed

Hooty needs a new home!
Finish the letter he is writing.
Use the Word Bank.

_____ Neighbors,
                1

I am a growing owl and I need a _____ home. If
                                          2

anyone _____ a tall tree with a big round
              3

_____ in it, please let me _____.
         4   5

I _____ really like a home that is shady and out of the
        6

_____. I stay out late, _____ I like to sleep
     7   8

during the day. In fact _____ days I do not wake until
                                9

_____ o'clock at night! If you think you have seen the
       10

perfect home _____ me, please give me a hoot.
                      11

I will be staying near the _____ for the next
                                    12

_____. Just look for the old _____ tree that
       13   14

is next to the_____ _____ bush.
                    15   16

Your friend,
Hooty

Word Bank

1. Deer/Dear	**5.** know/no	**9.** sum/some	**13.** week/weak
2. knew/new	**6.** would/wood	**10.** eight/ate	**14.** fur/fir
3. sees/seas	**7.** son/sun	**11.** four/for	**15.** red/read
4. hole/whole	**8.** sew/so	**12.** creak/creek	**16.** bury/berry

Bonus Box: On the back of this paper, draw and color a picture of the perfect new home for Hooty.

Name _____

Hanging Out

egg___
bush___
screech___
talon___
wing___
branch___
feather___
eye___
glass___
buzz___
fox___
beak___
owl___
class___
perch___
bird___

Add **es**
Add **s**

If a word ends in s, sh, ch, x, or z, add **es**.

Write **s** or **es** to make each word plural.
Write each plural word on a tree trunk.
Use the code to color each leaf.

Color Code
add **s** = red
add **es** = orange

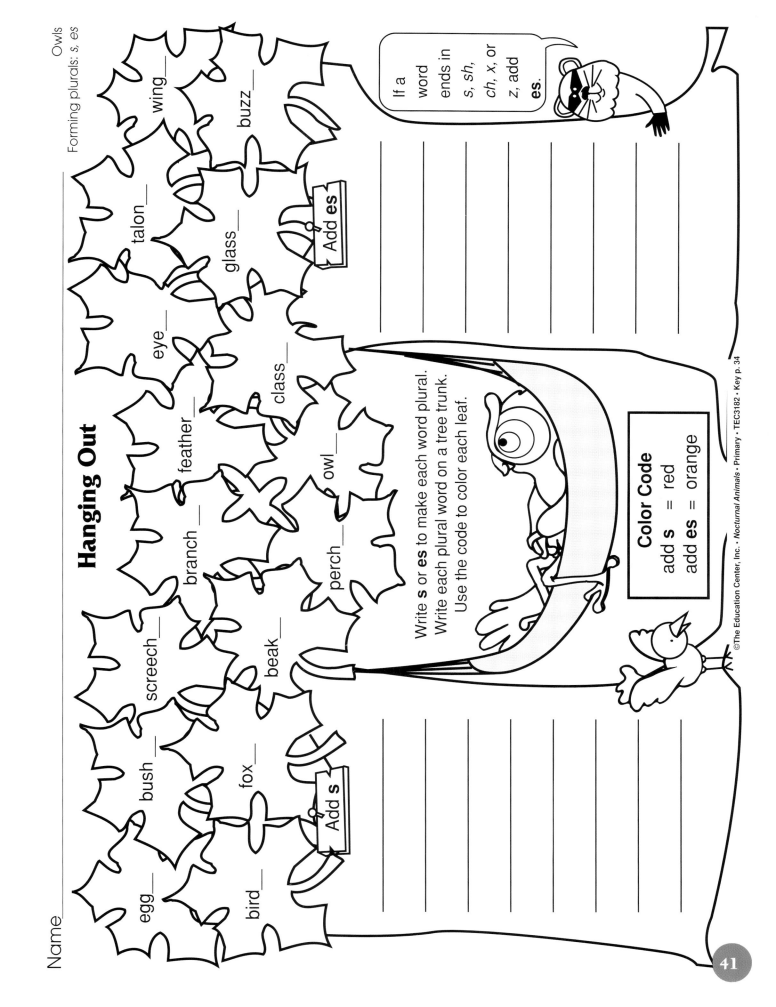

Background For The Teacher
Bats

There are more than 1,000 different kinds of bats in the world. These flying mammals come in all shapes and sizes, and live in all sorts of places. In fact, the only continent that bats do not inhabit is Antarctica. A bat's home or *roost* can be in a variety of places. Some bats live in caves, some live in treetops, and others live deep in hollow logs. Other bats roost in the nooks and crannies of castles, churches, and homes. Each bat may have a dozen or more places that it calls home.

There are two main groups of bats. *Microbats* is the larger of the two groups. Most of the 800 bat species in this group are small, insect-eating bats. The eyes of microbats are small, but they can probably see as well as mice. Microbats often have large ears and unusual-looking noses. The smaller bat group, called *megabats,* contains the larger bats. These large, fruit-eating bats (which resemble foxes) live mostly in the tropics of Asia and Africa. They have large eyes and see quite well. Unlike microbats, some megabats are active during the day.

Bats play an important role in the environment. Microbats are an effective and environmentally safe means of insect control. Megabats disperse seeds and pollinate plants that are very important to agriculture and forestry. Bat waste, called *guano,* is also a valuable fertilizer.

Related Literature
Bats

Zipping, Zapping, Zooming Bats (Let's-Read-And-Find-Out Science®) • Written by Ann Earle & Illustrated by Henry Cole • HarperCollins Children's Books, 1995

Extremely Weird: Bats • Written by Sarah Lovett with illustrations and photographs • John Muir Publications, 1995 (Distributed by Wright Group Publishing, Inc.)

Bats: Mysterious Flyers Of The Night • Written by Dee Stuart & Photographed by Merlin Tuttle • Carolrhoda Books, Inc.; 1994

Shadows Of Night: The Hidden World Of The Little Brown Bat • Written & Illustrated by Barbara Bash • Sierra Club Books, 1993

Answer Key For Page 43

1.	T	6.	T
2.	F	7.	T
3.	F	8.	F
4.	T	9.	T
5.	F	10.	F

Answer Key For Page 48

1. Daubenton's bat
2. false vampire bat, flying fox bat
3. five inches
4. big brown bat, red bat
5. hoary bat
6. five inches
7. bumblebee bat, little brown bat
8. Yes. Because the flying fox bat has a wingspan that is much larger than the big brown bat.

Brushing Up On Bats

Study the picture.
Read.

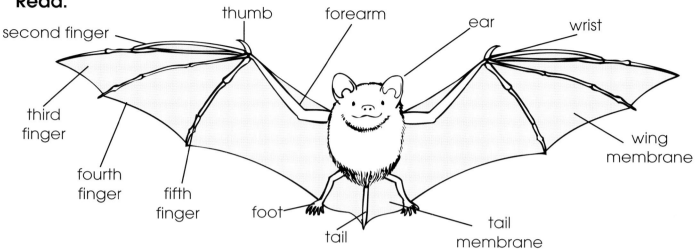

A bat is a mammal just like you. There are many kinds of bats. They come in all shapes and sizes. Bats have furry bodies. But they do not have fur on their wings. Did you know that bats have hands and feet? Bats have tails, too. Some bats have very strange-looking faces.

Bats sleep during the day. At night they come out to feed. Many bats eat insects. Some bats eat fruit. A few bats eat small animals like frogs or fish.

If the statement is true, write T on the line.
If the statement is false, write F on the line.

1. _____ Bats have legs.
2. _____ All bats look the same.
3. _____ Bats only eat insects.
4. _____ A bat has two wrists.
5. _____ Only a few bats have tails.

6. _____ Bats have fur.
7. _____ A bat has eight fingers and two thumbs.
8. _____ All bats eat the same things.
9. _____ Bats sleep during the day.
10. _____ Bats do not have feet.

Compare yourself to a bat.
Write two ways you are like a bat:

1. _____

2. _____

Write two ways you are not like a bat:

1. _____

2. _____

Materials Needed For Each Student:

— a copy of pages 45 and 47
— a white construction-paper copy of the bat booklet pattern below
— a pencil
— crayons or markers
— scissors
— access to a stapler

How To Use Pages 45 And 47 To Make A Bat Booklet

Distribute pages 45 and 47. Ask each student to color and personalize the booklet cover. Explain that each remaining booklet page needs an illustration. Read through the booklet pages together. Discuss each bat fact presented and brainstorm possible illustrations. Students may then proceed to illustrate their booklet pages independently.

How To Assemble The Bat Booklet

1. Color and cut out the bat booklet pattern. Set it aside.
2. Cutting on the heavy outlines, cut out the booklet cover and the 11 bookle pages on pages 45 and 47.
3. Stack the booklet cover and the booklet pages in sequential order; then staple the cover and the pages to the bat pattern where shown.

Bat Booklet Pattern

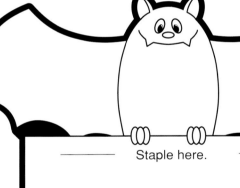

Staple here.

"Bat's" All, Folks!

The End

Bats are not blind. Their eyes are small, but they can see.

2.

Bats are amazing acrobats. They can swoop, twist, and turn.

5.

Bats are the only mammals that can fly.

1.

At night bats come out to feed.

4.

Bat Facts

by _____

©The Education Center, Inc.

During the day bats sleep hanging upside down.

3.

Brushing Up On Bats

How To Use This Page

To extend the booklet project described on page 44, give each student a copy of these patterns. Challenge each child to further research bats, then write and illustrate a different bat fact on each pattern. Each child then numbers and adds the resulting booklet pages to her booklet project.

To reinforce bat-related vocabulary, give each child three construction-paper copies of the patterns below and instructions for creating a Concentration game called Going Batty! To make the game, a child programs each of six cards with a different bat-related vocabulary word (like *roost, colony, nocturnal, pup,* etc.); then she writes the definition of each word on a blank card. Have each child store her resulting game cards in a resealable plastic bag. Provide time for student pairs to combine their cards and play the game they've created.

Open Bat Booklet Pages Or Game Cards

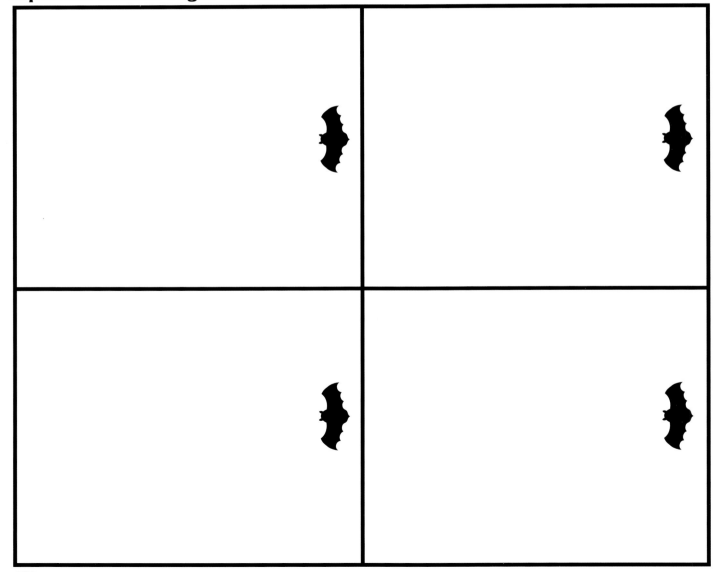

A few bats eat fish, frogs, and other small animals.

8.

Bats live in dark places. A bat home is called a *roost*.

11.

Some bats eat fruit.

7.

Bats use their calls to communicate and to hunt.

10.

Most bats eat insects. Some bats eat up to 600 mosquitoes an hour.

6.

Each kind of bat has its own call.

9.

Sizing Up Bats

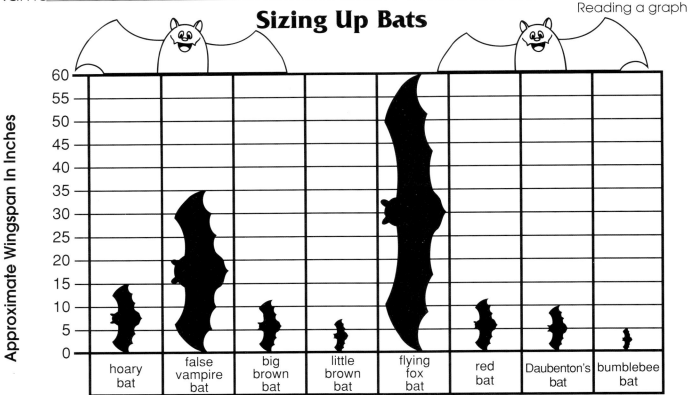

Answer the questions.
Use the graph.

1. Which bat has a wingspan of ten inches?_____

2. Which two bats have larger wingspans than the hoary bat?

   _____   _____

3. What is the wingspan of the bumblebee bat?_____

4. Which two bats have the same wingspan?

   _____   _____

5. Which bat has a wingspan that is larger than the big brown bat and smaller
   than the false vampire bat?_____

6. How many inches wider is the wingspan of the hoary bat than the
   Daubenton's bat? _____

7. Which two bats have the smallest wingspans?

   _____   _____

8. Do you think the flying fox bat weighs more than the big brown bat?_____
   Why? _____

   _____

48